WORKING AT A
MARINE
INSTITUTE

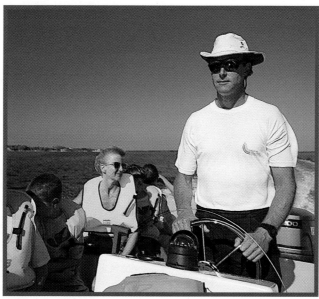

BY
WENDY DAVIS

ᑲᑭ Children's Press
A Division of Grolier Publishing
New York London Hong Kong Sydney
Danbury, Connecticut

Created and Developed by The Learning Source

Designed by Josh Simons, SimonSays Design!

Special thanks to Ginette Hughes at Marine Resources for her help and patience in the making of this book.

Photo Credits:
Marine Resources and Development Foundation: 2-3, 7 (inset), 8, 19, 21 (inset), 22, 24 (inset), 26, 28, 29, back cover; Tom & Therisa Stack/Tom Stack & Associates: Front Cover, 4-7, 9-18, 20-21, 23-25, 27.

Library of Congress Cataloging-in-Publication Data

Davis, Wendy.
Working at a marine institute / by Wendy Davis.
    p.   cm. -- (Working Here)
Includes bibliographical references and index.
Summary: Introduces some of the people who work at the Marine Resources Development Foundation in Florida, including field instructors, operations director, underwater researchers, and educational coordinator.
    ISBN 0-516-21223-0 (lib. bdg.)   0-516-26453-2 (pbk.)
    1. Marine resources development--Vocational guidance--Juvenile literature. 2. Marine Resources Development Foundation (Key Largo, Fla.) [1. Marine Resources Development Foundation (Key Largo. Fla.) 2. Marine sciences--Vocational guidance.   3. Occupations.]
I. Title.   II. Series.
GC1016.5.K56   1998
551.46'0072--dc21

                                                            98-13206

                        CIP

                        AC

Printed in the United States of America
1 2 3 4 5 6 7 8 9 10 R 06 05 04 03 02 01 00 99 98

For thousands of years, people have worked on and around the sea. But today, many people work under the sea, as well.

There are, for example, **geologists** who explore the sea's mountains and floor. There also are **archeologists** who pick through sunken wrecks and ruins. Still other **scientists** work under the sea to develop new foods and medicines.

For people interested in ocean science, a marine institute could be a fine place to work. Here, exploring a shipwreck, swimming with dolphins, or even studying tiny sea life can all be part of a day's work.

The Marine Resources Development Foundation is one of the best-known marine institutes in the world. It trains scientists to do research and other underwater work. It also helps people like you and me learn about life in the sea.

The institute runs two programs. The first is called Marine Lab, which is a hands-on learning environment. Here, groups of children or adults get to explore everything from mangrove swamps to coral reefs.

Most of the people who work at Marine Lab do more than one job. The **director**, for example, supervises the workers and keeps the program running smoothly. He even welcomes new students as they arrive.

Marine Lab's **education coordinator** chooses the subjects that visiting students will study. She also handles **public relations**, letting outsiders know all about Marine Lab and its work.

Another important job belongs to the **operations director**. He is in charge of many of Marine Lab's day-to-day activities. He teaches water safety, captains the boats, and supervises almost everything that happens on and under the water.

The staff members that students see most often are called **field instructors**. Most of these instructors have studied marine biology. Their main job is to teach the students about the sea and its life forms.

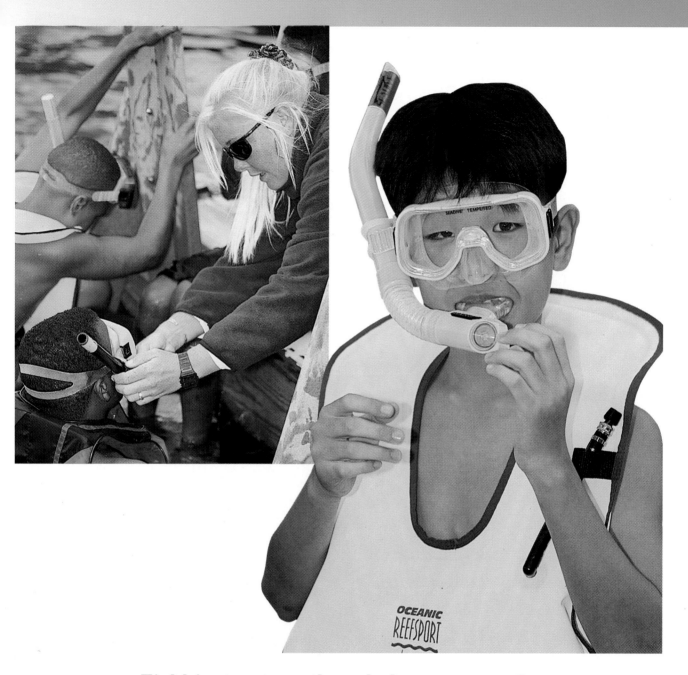

Field instructors, though, have many other tasks. All new students must be able to see what is going on under the water. It is up to Marine Lab's instructors to show everyone how to use the snorkel, mask, and flippers.

Instructors also lead students on underwater journeys of discovery. Along the way these instructors answer questions and provide information about everything around them.

But field instructors are not in the water all the time. Many, in fact, spend part of their work day in classrooms. There, they help students learn even more about life in the sea.

Instructors also work as **mechanics**, keeping Marine Lab's boats and underwater gear in top working order. Some instructors become good enough to repair even the most complicated equipment.

Beneath the surface of a nearby lagoon is the institute's other program. It is an undersea training center called The Man in the Sea. This is where **oceanographers**, **researchers**, and other scientists learn how to carry out underwater jobs.

Most of the teachers in the Man in the Sea program are **aquanauts**—very experienced underwater divers. In fact, anyone who even takes part in this program must have at least some SCUBA experience.

The word SCUBA stands for Self-Contained Underwater Breathing Apparatus. This special equipment allows divers to breathe under the water and roam around freely, almost like fish.

With the help of an Exo-mask like this one, divers can even talk with one another while they are under the water.

The aquanauts lead the scientists on model projects. Soon they are able to gather samples, map the ocean floor, or even dive at night.

Some of these students need to master more advanced equipment, like the diving bell and the mini-sub.

A diving bell takes aquanauts and students deeper than SCUBA divers usually go. It protects divers from water pressure, cold temperatures, and even dangerous sea creatures.

The program's mini-sub holds just one person at a time. A student who learns how to use it can safely explore the ocean floor.

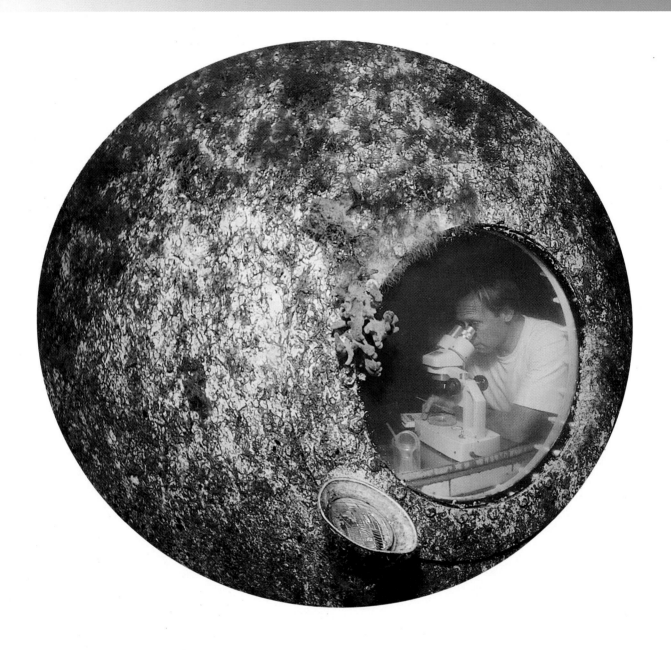

This undersea laboratory is used for longer training sessions. With the aquanauts' help, students of the program soon master the art of living and working in this underwater research station.

Visitors can stay overnight in the underwater hotel. It has everything found at home, except that it is located 30 feet (9 meters) below the water's surface. As long as visitors stay inside the hotel, no breathing equipment is needed.

Of course the institute has other workers, too. Without the **food staff**, who would cook the meals? And without **bookkeepers** and **accountants**, who would pay the bills for food or equipment?

The environment beneath the sea has been called Earth's last great frontier. Like astronauts exploring outer space, aquanauts and undersea scientists are also discovering a new and wonderful world.

Perhaps one day, you too will choose to make the sea the center of your work. If so, you may find yourself **working here** at a marine institute like this one.

Taking a Closer Look

Page 4

There are more than 2,600 kinds of palm trees. Most have a branchless trunk with a crown of leaves at the top. In some cases, these leaves grow to 65 feet (20 meters) long and 8 feet (2.4 meters) wide.

Page 8

Coral is a limestone formation made by millions of tiny animals. Some coral can look like giant brains, others like columns or pillars. What you see here is called antler coral. Can you tell why?

Page 5

Geologists are scientists who study the rocks that make up the earth's crust. Archeologists are scientists who study the bones, buildings, and other objects of ancient people to see how they once lived.

Page 8

Mangrove trees grow in ocean water. A mangrove sends many roots from its branches down into the water. Soon, hundreds of roots that look like stilts support the leafy top.

Page 7

Divers sometimes carry waterproof cards to help them identify different kinds of sea life. This diver has just come across a sea fan, which is a type of coral.

Page 12

The large white object in the photo is a personnel transfer capsule. It is used to bring scientists from the surface down to underwater labs where they will stay and do deep-sea research.

Page 13

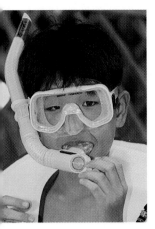

A face mask allows a swimmer to see clearly under the water. With a snorkel, a swimmer is able to breathe while floating face down on the water's surface. Rubber fins make it easier to swim faster and longer.

Page 19

A SCUBA diver breathes in air through a mouthpiece. The air comes from one or two metal tanks strapped onto the diver's back. The air flows from the tanks through tubes and then into the mouthpiece.

Page 17

A lagoon is a shallow body of water that is connected to a larger body such as the sea. What separates the two is often a coral reef or a sandy strip of land.

Page 23

Diving bells lower aquanauts deep into the ocean so they can collect samples, observe rare fish, or carry out other tasks. Some diving bells go as far down as 800 feet (240 meters).

Page 17

The clear, plastic bubble on the underwater lab was once part of the U.S. Navy sub *Nemo*. It was designed to give a wide-range view of the surrounding ocean.

Page 24

The mini-sub is a tiny version of a full-sized submarine. As small as it is, though, it can dive down to 300 feet (90 meters) and provide life support for up to 72 hours.

Index

accountants, 27

aquanauts , 18, 21, 23, 25, 28

archeologists, 5

bookkeepers, 27

classrooms, 15

coral reefs, 8

director, 9
   operations, 11
   public relations, 10

diver, 18, 19, 20

diving bell, 22, 23

education coordinator, 10

Exo-mask, 20

field instructors, 12, 13

flippers, 13

food staff, 27

geologists, 5

laboratory, 25

mangrove swamps, 8

Man in the Sea, 17, 18

marine biology, 12

marine institute, 6, 7, 29

Marine Lab, 8-11, 13, 16, 27

Marine Resources and
Development Foundation, 7

mask, 13

mechanics, 16

mini-sub, 22, 24

oceanographers, 17

researchers, 17

scientists, 5, 7, 17, 21, 28

sea, 4-7, 12, 15, 23, 28, 29

snorkel, 13

student(s), 9, 10, 12-15, 22-25

SCUBA , 18, 19, 23

underwater hotel, 26